# Destination Detectives

WITHDRAWN FROM STOCK

# France

EXPRESS EDITION

North America

Europe

Asia

FRANCE

Africa

South America

Australasia

Paul Mason

**www.raintreepublishers.co.uk**
Visit our website to find out more information about **Raintree** books.

To order:
☎ Phone 44 (0) 1865 888112
📄 Send a fax to 44 (0) 1865 314091
💻 Visit the Raintree Bookshop at **www.raintreepublishers.co.uk** to browse our catalogue and order online.

First published in Great Britain by
Raintree, Halley Court, Jordan Hill,
Oxford OX2 8EJ, part of Harcourt Education.
Raintree is a registered trademark of Harcourt
Education Ltd.

Produced for Raintree Publishers by Discovery Books Ltd
Editorial: Kathryn Walker, Melanie Copland, and Lucy Beevor
Design: Victoria Bevan, Rob Norridge, and Kamae Design
Picture Research: Hannah Taylor and Kay Altwegg
Production: Duncan Gilbert
Originated by Modern Age
Printed and bound in China
by South China Printing Company

10 digit ISBN 1 406 20400 5 (hardback)
13 digit ISBN 978 1 406 20400 1
10 09 08 07 06
10 9 8 7 6 5 4 3 2 1

10 digit ISBN 1 406 2040 72 (paperback)
13 digit ISBN 978 1 406 20407 0
10 09 08 07 06
10 9 8 7 6 5 4 3 2 1

**British Library Cataloguing in Publication Data**
Mason, Paul
France. – (Destination detectives)
944'.084
A full catalogue record for this book is available from
the British Library.

This levelled text is a version of *Freestyle:
Destination Detectives: France*

**Acknowledgements**
Alamy Images pp. 9 (Agence Images), 35 (Directphoto.org),
34r (images-of-france), 6b (Jack Sullivan), 41 (Jon Arnold
Images), 20 (Justin Kase), 13 (mediacolors), 32 (Nick
Hanna), 10 (Travel Ink), 7 (Westend61); Anthony Blake
Photo Library pp. 16–17 (Gerrit Buntrock), 17 (Robert
Golden); Corbis pp. 18–19 (Bryan F. Peterson), pp. 24r, 26
(Chris Lisle), 33 (Dave G. Houser), 37 (Emmanuelle
Thiercelin), 39 (Gail Mooney), 12–13 (Galen Rowell), 27
(Nik Wheeler), 43 (Owen Franken), 30 (Philip Gould), pp. 4,
4–5 (PicImpact), pp. 5m, 15, 36, 42 (Reuters), 40t (Sally A.
Morgan; Ecoscene), 25 (Sylvain Saustier), 34l (Thomas
Hartwell), pp. 11, 28–29 (Yann Arthus-Bertrand); Corbis
Sygma pp. 21 (John Van Hasselt), 14 (P. Franck); Getty
Images pp. 5b, 24l, 29 (Photodisc), 42–43 (Stone); Harcourt
Education Ltd p. 23 (Paul Mason); Rex Features pp. 18,
30–31 (Sipa Press); Robert Harding pp. 38 (David Hughes),
6t (Travel Library), pp. 5t, 8 (Roy Rainford), 40 (Ruth
Tomlinson), 22 (Sylvain Grandadam).

Cover photograph of an unusual angle of the Eiffel Tower
reproduced with permission from Getty Images/Photodisc.

Every effort has been made to contact copyright
holders of any material reproduced in this book.
Any omissions will be rectified in subsequent
printings if notice is given to the publishers.

The paper used to print this book comes from
sustainable resources.

# Contents

Any words appearing in the text in bold, **like this,** are explained in the glossary. You can also look out for them in the Word Bank at the bottom of each page.

# Where in the world?

## Skiing in the French Alps

Skiing is very popular in the French Alps (see below). Between December and April, millions of people go there to ski. Some stay there for the whole winter.

You wake up to the sound of cowbells. You open the shutters of your window. In front of you is a sloping meadow. It is surrounded by woods.

To your left, the slope drops down. In the distance you see a little town at the bottom of a **valley**. To your right, the slope climbs and climbs. It rises so high that you cannot see the top. You are in the mountains. But what country is it?

**WORD BANK**   valley  area of lowland between hills or mountains

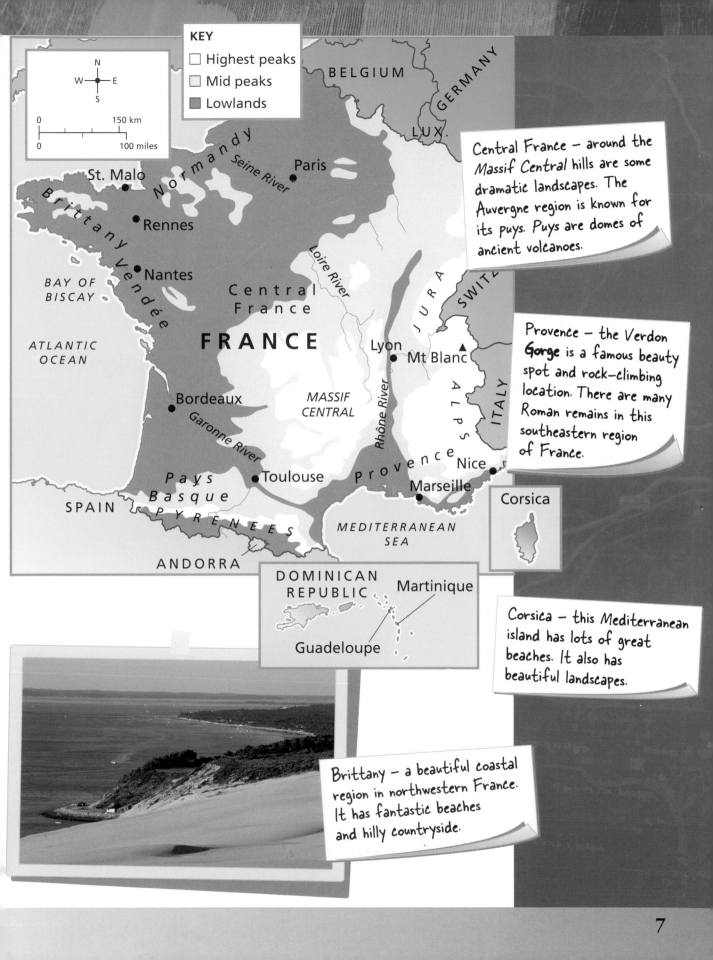

KEY
- ☐ Highest peaks
- ☐ Mid peaks
- ▨ Lowlands

N
W E
S

0   150 km
0   100 miles

BELGIUM

GERMANY

LUX.

Normandy

St. Malo

Paris

Seine River

Brittany

Rennes

Vendée

Nantes

BAY OF
BISCAY

Central
France

Loire River

JURA

SWITZ

ATLANTIC
OCEAN

**FRANCE**

Lyon

▲ Mt Blanc

Bordeaux

Garonne River

MASSIF
CENTRAL

Rhône River

ALPS

ITALY

Pays
Basque

Toulouse

Provence

Nice

SPAIN

PYRENEES

Marseille

Corsica

ANDORRA

MEDITERRANEAN
SEA

DOMINICAN
REPUBLIC

Martinique

Guadeloupe

Central France – around the Massif Central hills are some dramatic landscapes. The Auvergne region is known for its puys. Puys are domes of ancient volcanoes.

Provence – the Verdon **Gorge** is a famous beauty spot and rock-climbing location. There are many Roman remains in this southeastern region of France.

Corsica – this Mediterranean island has lots of great beaches. It also has beautiful landscapes.

Brittany – a beautiful coastal region in northwestern France. It has fantastic beaches and hilly countryside.

# The French landscape

You are staying in a house called a **chalet**. A chalet is a type of house often found in the Alps. It is made of wood. Outside, the Alps tower over you. They are Europe's highest mountains. The tallest mountain in the Alps is Mont Blanc. This name means "White Mountain". Mont Blanc's upper slopes are always covered in snow.

The French Alps form part of the **border** between France and Italy.

PARIS

You are here!

ALPS

N
W · E
S

0   150 km

0   100 miles

## Mont Blanc

**HEIGHT:**
4,807 metres
(15,771 feet)

**FIRST CLIMBED:**
by Michel Paccard
and Jacques
Balmat in 1786

**PEOPLE KILLED
CLIMBING:**
over 1,000 people
by 2004

This is the peak of Europe's tallest mountain, Mont Blanc.

  border imaginary line dividing one country from another

## Other French mountains

North-west of the French Alps lie the Jura Mountains (see map, page 7). The Jura lie along the border between France and Switzerland.

West of the Alps is the Massif Central. These highlands are the remains of ancient volcanoes. The volcanoes have been worn down by the weather.

In south-west France, the Pyrenees mountains separate France and Spain. Some of the biggest peaks here are over 3,000 metres (10,000 feet).

### Alpine animals

The Alps are home to some rare animals. They include a type of mountain antelope called the chamois. There is also a long-horned mountain goat called the ibex. High up in the Alps, golden eagles and lammergeier vultures make their nests.

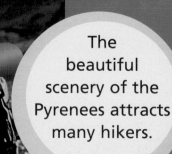

The beautiful scenery of the Pyrenees attracts many hikers.

## Little streams and great rivers

There are little streams everywhere in these mountains. They all join up in the **valleys**. Then they turn into fast-flowing rivers. These rivers attract **kayakers** and **white-water rafters**.

## The Rhône

Many Alpine rivers (rivers of the Alps) empty into the River Rhône. The Rhône begins in the Swiss Alps and flows into the Mediterranean Sea. It carries more water than any other French river.

**France's longest rivers:**

**Rhône:**
480 kilometres
(300 miles)

**Garonne:**
500 kilometres
(310 miles)

**Seine:**
770 kilometres
(480 miles)

**Loire:**
1,020 kilometres
(630 miles).

In spring, white-water rafters head for the rivers of the Alps. This is when the snow melts. Melting snow fills the rivers with fast-moving water.

kayaker someone who paddles a small, light boat like a canoe through water

### The Garonne

The Garonne river starts life in the Pyrenees mountains (see map, page 7). It flows past the cities of Toulouse and Bordeaux.

### The River Seine

The Seine is France's most famous river. It flows through the capital city, Paris. The Seine was once an important transport route to and from the city.

### The River Loire

The Loire is France's longest river. It flows from the Massif Central in south-central France to the Atlantic Ocean.

The Seine flows through the city of Paris. The small island in the river seen here is the *Ile de la Cité* ("Island of the City"). It is the city's historic centre.

white-water rafter  someone who paddles or rows a raft along a fast-moving river with a strong current

# Weather in France

The Alps are mostly sunny and warm during summer. But the weather here can suddenly change. The heat, high mountains, and damp air allows thunderstorms to build up very quickly. The thunderclaps boom along the **valleys.** A drenching downpour follows.

You are likely to meet people of all ages while you are out hiking.

**WORD BANK**  industry  businesses that provide a particular service

# Tourist attraction

Many people visit the Alps all through the year. They come to ski, to walk, to climb, and to go biking. Tourism is the biggest **industry**, or business, in this region.

You notice lots of ski lifts on the mountainsides. In summer they sometimes take walkers and mountain bikers to the higher slopes. The snows begin in November or December. Then the lifts carry skiers up the mountains.

## Holiday fun

*Hydro-glisse*: swimming down a fast-flowing river holding a special float.

**White-water rafting:** six people paddle or row a boat along fast-moving rivers.

**Canyoning:** climbing, jumping, and **abseiling** (descending on ropes) down waterfalls.

**Mountain biking:** brilliant fun on the summer bike trails.

► This canyoner is hoping for a soft landing!

**abseiling** using climbing rope to come down a steep hill or cliff face

## Temperatures in France

Look at the map and table below. The table tells you what the average temperatures are around France in February and August.

## Wet and windy north

What is the weather like in other parts of France? Northern France can be freezing, wet, and windy in winter. It is sometimes wet and windy in summer too.

## Warmer south

The south coast of France has hot, dry summers. The average temperature in midsummer is about 24 °C (75 °F). Even in winter the temperature rarely dips below 8 °C (46 °F).

| City | February | | August | |
|------|----------|--|--------|--|
| Lyon | 6.7 °C | (44.1 °F) | 27.6 °C | (81.7°F) |
| Nice | 12.0 °C | (53.6 °F) | 28.4 °C | (83.1 °F) |
| Paris | 7.0 °C | (44.6 °F) | 25.6 °C | (78.0 °F) |
| St. Malo | 8.6 °C | (47.5 °F) | 24.0 °C | (75.2 °F) |
| Strasbourg | 5.3 °C | (41.5 °F) | 26.3 °C | (79.3 °F) |
| Toulouse | 1.5 °C | (34.7 °F) | 28.0 °C | (82.4 °F) |

> During winter, parts of northern and western France can be very windy, grey, and cold!

## Eastern climate

Eastern France has cold winters and hot summers. The city of Strasbourg is right on France's eastern border. Here the winter temperature is often below freezing. But summer temperatures can climb above 24 °C (75 °F).

## Wet in the west

The weather in the west is affected by the Atlantic Ocean. In winter big storms move in from the sea. In summer the beaches are packed with people enjoying the sunshine.

### Heatwave 2003

In 2003, France suffered one of its worst **heatwaves**:

- temperatures rose to over 40 °C (104 °F)
- crops dried up in the fields
- the deaths of up to 13,000 people were linked to the extreme heat.

A forest fire in La Motte, southern France, was probably started by a campfire. Because of the heatwave, the fire spread many miles. ◄

# Eating and drinking

Walking in the mountains has made you hungry. You could go to one of the snack or sandwich bars. Or there are cafés where you can sit indoors or outside. For a bigger meal, there are restaurants.

If you decide on a sit-down meal, you could try one of the local dishes. In the Alps, these often contain dried meats, cheese, potatoes, and onions.

Eating out is popular in France. On average, people eat away from home every 3 days.

# Eating habits

Traditional French meals can last a long time. You might start with soup, followed by fish. Next there may be meat followed by dessert. A meal often ends with cheese.

Today, people might have this traditional type of meal on a special occasion. This could be a festival or a family visit. On an ordinary day, people usually have a quick snack for lunch.

## Alpine specials:

*Raclette*: special cheese melted on boiled potatoes

*Pierre Chaude*: a bag of boiled potatoes, raw meats, and a hot rock to cook on!

*Fondue*: (see below) melted cheese for dipping meats or vegetables

*Tartiflette*: a baked pastry dish with cheese, bacon, and onion.

# Travelling in France

## Terror in the tunnel

The Mont Blanc tunnel links France to Italy by road. In March 1999, a fire started in the tunnel. At least 30 cars were trapped and 39 people died. The tunnel did not reopen until 2002.

This is a **memorial** to the 39 people who died in the Mont Blanc tunnel disaster.

The Alps are beautiful, but it's time to visit some other places. From the French Alps you can reach Italy or Switzerland very quickly.

But you want to stay in France. You decide to head for the capital. The capital is Paris. It is in the centre of northern France. How will you get there?

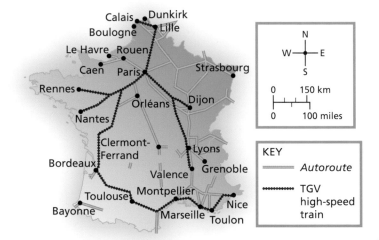

KEY

—— *Autoroute*

········ TGV high-speed train

TGV (*train à grande vitesse*) French high-speed train

# Fast trains

Leaving the Alps by road is easy. But the wiggly mountain roads can take a long time. The quickest way to reach Paris is probably to take a **TGV** train.

TGV stands for *train à grande vitesse*. This means "high speed train". TGV trains can reach speeds of 300 kilometres (185 miles) per hour. They run between many of France's main cities (see map on page 18). The journey to Paris takes you just over 4 hours.

## The Métro

Paris's **Métro** (underground train system) opened in 1900. It now has 14 lines. No point in the city is more than 500 metres (546 yards) away from a Métro station.

TGV trains link France's biggest cities. They form part of a high-speed train network that covers much of Europe.

## Dangerous roads

France's roads are twice as dangerous as roads in the United Kingdom or the United States. This is mainly because of the heavy traffic during August. August is when people either go to, or return from, their traditional month-long holiday.

# Getting about

France has an excellent transport system. The train service is good. It is also easy to get about by car or aeroplane.

# On the road

For long-distance car journeys, many people use the roads called *autoroutes*. These are faster than most other roads. People have to pay to use *autoroutes*. This means there is usually less traffic on them. For shorter journeys, most drivers use smaller roads.

Traffic builds up near the Arc de Triomphe, Paris's famous arch. Heavy traffic is a problem in many French towns and cities.

## Tunnel under the sea

France is connected to the United Kingdom by the **Channel Tunnel**. The tunnel runs under the **English Channel**. The Channel is a narrow stretch of the Atlantic that separates France from the United Kingdom. Trains carry cars and passengers through the tunnel.

## Jetting around

All the big cities in France have large airports. Travellers arrive at them from many parts of the world. There are also lots of smaller airports around the country.

Cars drive off a Channel Tunnel train. The Channel Tunnel links England and France. It first opened in 1994.

**Channel Tunnel** railway tunnel under the English Channel

# Countryside and coast

## Life in the countryside

You see some beautiful countryside on your way to Paris. Your train passes through the Burgundy region. This is where some of the most famous wine in the world is made.

South-west of Burgundy is the area of Limousin. The countryside here is hilly and wooded. It is not good for farming. It is very beautiful here. People from other countries buy homes in Burgundy to enjoy the beauty.

> In the 19th century a plant disease destroyed most of the ancient grapevines in Burgundy. Many of those vines had been planted during Roman times.

**WORD BANK**    Basque people who live on the slopes of the Pyrenees mountains. They have their own language and way of life.

# New arrivals

Some wealthy foreigners buy homes in France. Many of these people are from the United Kingdom (or UK). This is because houses in France cost less than in many other countries. Also, France is warmer than the United Kingdom.

In some parts of France this is causing problems. Foreign buyers have pushed up the prices of houses. Some local people can no longer afford to buy their own houses.

## The Basques

The **Basque** people live in south-west France. Many Basques also live across the **border** in Spain. The Basque language is called *Euskera*. This is a very difficult language for travellers to learn.

You may see the sign "à *vendre*" many times on your trip. It means "for sale".

border imaginary line dividing one country from another

## Farming

Burgundy is one of the richest areas in France. But other parts of the French countryside are poor. Many farmers make very little money.

Today, less than 10 percent of the population works in farming. Most French people work in towns and cities. Many of them live in the countryside but travel to work.

### "Local" bananas

The bananas you buy in France might have travelled thousands of miles to get there. But they may still be French! This is because the Caribbean islands of Martinique and Guadeloupe (see map on page 7) belong to France.

Provence in south-east France is a famous producer of lavender.

## Types of farm

Nearly 60 percent of France is used for farming. Most of the large farms grow crops such as cereal. Medium-sized farms often concentrate on farming animals.

The small farms usually produce crops such as grapes for making wine. Often, the small farmers do not work full-time on their farms. They can only make a living by doing another job as well.

## Frogs' legs

Frogs' legs are a traditional French dish. Farms in France produce millions of frogs each year for eating.

◄ Huge fields are used to grow large amounts of food in France.

## Farming seafood!

French farmers do not only raise crops or animals. Some raise seafood. They grow it in the water though, not in fields! In 1999 French fish farmers produced more than 300 million kilograms (660 million pounds) of **seafood**.

Seafood is becoming more and more popular in France. The French now eat almost twice as much fish as they did 20 years ago.

## What's on the menu?

These are some of the dishes that you might find on restaurant menus in France:

**Starter:**
*Assiette anglaise*: plate of cold meats

*Consommé:* clear, well-seasoned soup

**Fish:**
*Langoustine à l'aïoli:* crayfish (see right) with garlic mayonnaise

*Moules marinières*: mussels, cooked with shallots (little onions) in white wine.

Fishermen on a small trawler gather in buckets of crayfish to sell to local markets.

seafood fish, such as cod, and shellfish, such as crabs and mussels

## Fishing in the sea

France has 2,543 kilometres (1,580 miles) of coastline. There are fishing boats all along the coast. Most of these are small boats. They are used to fish in the waters close to the shore. Owners of the boats often take the fish catch to market themselves.

## Lakes and rivers

Freshwater fish are also popular in France. Carp, salmon, trout, and bass are all fished in France's rivers and lakes.

### More dishes

**Meat:**

*Coq au vin*: chicken cooked with wine, mushrooms, and onions

*Boeuf bourguignon*: beef stew with red wine, onions, and mushrooms

**Dessert:**

*Bombe*: layers of ice cream shaped in a rounded mould

*Crêpe Suzette*: thin pancake with a sweet orange sauce.

Most French fish farms raise shellfish as well. In total, they produce 30 times more shellfish than fish.

# Life in the cities

PARIS

You are here!

N
W — E
S

0    150 km

0    100 miles

The **TGV** train rolls into the Gare de Lyon station. You are now in Paris, the capital of France. From the Gare de Lyon you can catch a **Métro** train to anywhere in the city. Where do you want to go first?

## Le Parkour

*Le Parkour* is an activity that started in Paris. It involves running, leaping, and climbing high up among the rooftops. *Le Parkour* features in movies and adverts.

**WORD BANK**    Métro Paris underground train system

## Paris choices

You could wander around the narrow old streets of the Marais district. You might visit Notre Dame church. This was the setting for the famous story *The Hunchback of Notre Dame*. There is so much to see and do here.

## Ups and downs

Paris has great museums and art galleries. It also has excellent restaurants and markets. Paris is a very beautiful city. But it does have some problems. Heavy traffic causes **pollution**. Also, there are areas of **poverty** on the edge of Paris.

During the 1800s, much of Paris was rebuilt. The city was organized around wide streets called *boulevards*.

### The Eiffel Tower

**Built:** 1889

**Height:** 300 metres (985 feet). When it was built, it was the tallest structure in the world.

**History:** The Eiffel Tower was meant to be torn down after 20 years. But it was used as a giant radio aerial instead.

poverty  lack of money, a good home, or enough to eat

# Going to school

You decide to climb to the top of the Eiffel Tower. The scene from its viewing platform is amazing. You can see right across the city.

There are crowds of children up on the viewing platform. You chat with them. They tell you what school is like in France.

This boy in Guadeloupe cycles to class wearing shorts and a T-shirt. The weather in Guadeloupe is warm throughout the year.

Everyone in France has to go to school between the ages of six and sixteen. Children go to primary school until they are ten years old. Then they go to *collège* until they are sixteen.

## Lycée

After *collège*, some students study for another three years. They go to the *lycée*. One type of *lycée* trains people for particular jobs. A second type is for those learning science or technology. The third type of *lycée* prepares students for university.

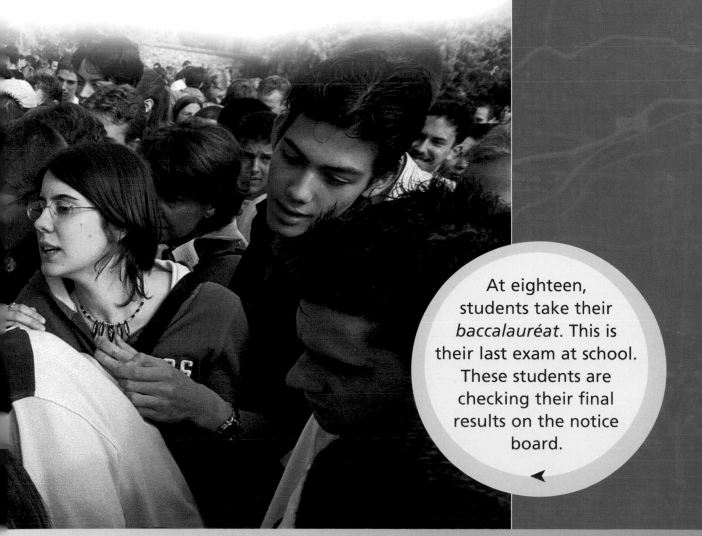

At eighteen, students take their *baccalauréat*. This is their last exam at school. These students are checking their final results on the notice board.

## French cities

From Paris you could travel to any other French city. Where will you go next?

Nantes — Visit the *Musée d'Histoire Naturelle* (Natural History Museum). You can see rhinoceros toenails and an Egyptian mummy, among other things!

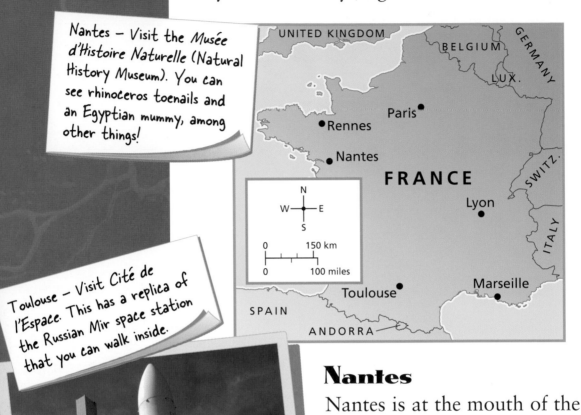

Toulouse — Visit Cité de l'Espace. This has a replica of the Russian Mir space station that you can walk inside.

UNITED KINGDOM
BELGIUM
GERMANY
LUX.
Paris
Rennes
Nantes
FRANCE
SWITZ.
Lyon
ITALY
N
W E
S
0    150 km
0    100 miles
Toulouse
Marseille
SPAIN
ANDORRA

## Nantes

Nantes is at the mouth of the Loire River. It is in western France. This city grew rich from trade and shipbuilding.

## Toulouse

Toulouse is in south-west France. This is a modern city with an ancient centre. Toulouse is known for its space and aircraft **industries**. Businesses that produce aircraft, rockets, and satellites are based here.

Lyon – Take the funicular train up Fourvière Hill. There you can visit the town's Roman remains.

## Marseille

This Mediterranean port has been a trading base for 2,500 years. One quarter of Marseille's population are either from North Africa or are children of North Africans.

Marseille – Visit the spooky burial chambers called **catacombs**. These are in the Basilique St-Victor. This is the town's oldest church.

## Lyon

Lyon is in east-central France. It was once a famous silk-making centre. After World War II, other industries became important.

Rennes – visit Les Lices. This is the tiny bit of ancient Rennes that survived the 1720 fire.

## Rennes

Rennes is in north-west France. A fire burned down most of the city in 1720. Today, Rennes is a trading centre. It is also the capital of Brittany.

catacombs   tunnels used as burial chambers

## City life

About 75 percent of French people live in cities. What is life like for them? In some ways it is like city life in many other countries.

## Good things

There are many reasons why people choose to live in France's cities:

- there are plenty of jobs based in the cities
- there are great shops and restaurants
- there are sports halls, art galleries, and museums
- there are cinemas and theatres.

## Bands to see

Many **immigrants** have come to live in French cities. Immigrants are people who have arrived from other countries. They have brought new music to France.

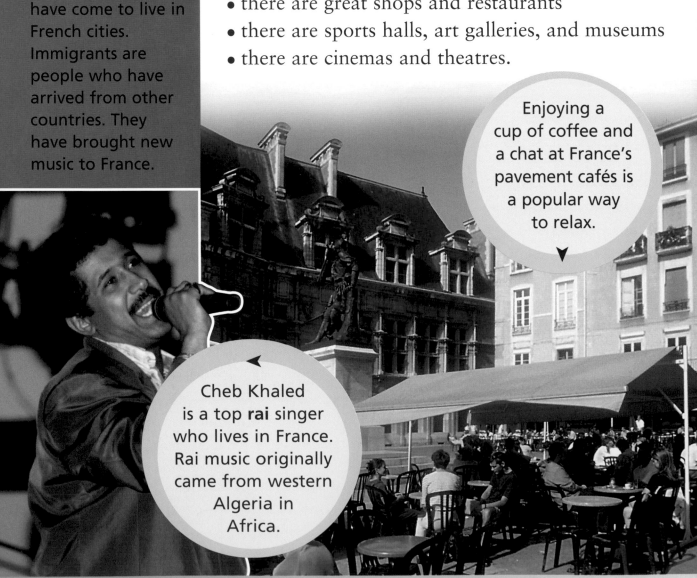

Enjoying a cup of coffee and a chat at France's pavement cafés is a popular way to relax.

Cheb Khaled is a top **rai** singer who lives in France. Rai music originally came from western Algeria in Africa.

immigrant someone who originally comes from a different country

## Not-so-good things

Of course, there are also problems with city life:

- most people live in apartments instead of houses. These apartments tend to be small.
- buying or renting a home can be expensive.
- traffic can be a problem. Noise and **pollution** from cars fills the air. Some cities are divided by busy highways.

## Le Weekend

French people who live in cities like to get away for *Le Weekend* (Saturday and Sunday). In summer, many families like to go camping in the countryside.

French people love to escape the city for a weekend's camping.

rai type of music originally from western Algeria

# Sport and culture

## Tour de France

The Tour de France bike race is one of France's most popular events. It is run every year in July. The race always finishes at Paris's famous Arc de Triomphe (see picture on right).

American rider Lance Armstrong is seen here in the Tour de France. Armstrong has won the Tour de France seven times. No-one else has ever done this.

**WORD BANK**   voyage   long journey

## Popular sports

People throughout France enjoy cycling, skiing, and tennis. Football and rugby are also very popular. They are played and watched with great excitement.

## Distance racing

Long-distance races, such as the Tour de France bike race, are very popular in France. French people particularly love long-distance yacht races.

The toughest yacht race is the Vendée Globe race. The racers sail around the world without stopping. They have to sail alone and have no help. The fastest boats take about 90 days to make the **voyage**.

The Vendée Globe race begins and ends at the port of Les Sables d'Olonne on the west coast of France.

These are the days when most people in France have a day off. Many of them are Christian holidays.

**1 JANUARY**
New Year's Day

**EASTER SUNDAY** and **EASTER MONDAY**

**ASCENSION DAY**
40 days after Easter

**PENTECOST**
the seventh Sunday after Easter

**1 MAY**   May Day

**8 MAY**   Victory in Europe (VE) Day. This celebrates the end of World War II in Europe.

## Visit the Louvre

The Louvre in Paris is one of the world's greatest museums. Its most famous exhibit is a painting called the *Mona Lisa*. This was painted by a great Italian artist named Leonardo da Vinci.

## Go to the cinema

About half the films shown in France are foreign. Most of them are from the United States. But the French make many of their own films too. Some French films are big hits all around the world.

➤ This fantastic glass building is called *La Pyramide*. It stands beside the Louvre Museum in Paris.

**revolution**   replacing a government with a new one, usually by force

## See theatre, dance, or music

France has many theatres. People go there to see plays, dance, or music performances. There's usually lots of types of music performed, particularly in Paris.

In summertime, street theatre is popular. Actors perform outdoors. When they have finished, the actors pass round a hat. People who enjoyed the performance put in some money.

**More holidays**

**14 JULY** Bastille Day, remembering the French **Revolution**

**15 AUGUST** Assumption Day

**1 NOVEMBER** All Saints' Day

**11 NOVEMBER** Armistice Day. This celebrates the end of World War I.

**25 DECEMBER** Christmas Day

**31 DECEMBER** New Year's Eve.

These two actors are part of a street theatre performance.

39

# Tourist hot spots

On the **Métro** you find a map that someone has left on the next seat. It shows some of France's top tourist attractions.

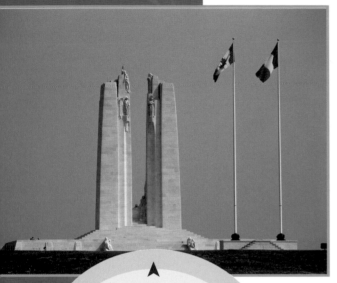

## Battlefields of World War I

Between 1914 and 1918, World War I raged in northern France. Today visitors can walk where the battles were fought.

This war **memorial** stands in northern France. It was built to remember Canadian soldiers who died in the Battle of Arras during World War I.

**WORD BANK**     abbey     building used by people who belong to a religious order

# The Verdon Gorge

The Verdon **Gorge** is an amazing **canyon** in southeastern France (see bottom of page 40). This is one of the most beautiful parts of France.

# Carnac

Carnac is a town in Brittany in north-west France. It is famous for the thousands of ancient stones that stand in lines across the land.

# Mont St Michel

Mont St Michel is a rocky island off the northwestern coast of France. It is home to a famous **abbey** (religious meeting place). This abbey is shown in the picture on the right.

# Lascaux cave paintings

Some of the world's oldest paintings are on cave walls in Lascaux in southern France. The paintings were discovered in 1940 by four boys who followed a dog into a cave.

> Mont St Michel used to be cut off from the mainland at high tide. Many people drowned trying to reach the abbey.

# Stay, or go home?

You have been to the Alps and you have crossed the centre of France. You have explored Paris. During your time in France, you have found out about how French people live. You now know what they eat and how they like to enjoy themselves.

## Learn to surf in Hossegor

Hossegor is the capital of French surfing. This coastal resort is in south-west France. Every year a world surfing championship is held at Hossegor. But there are easy waves for beginners, too!

Brazilian championship surfer Jacqueline Silva surfs the huge waves in the Hossegor world championships.

**WORD BANK**   truffle   fleshy fungus that grows underground or around the roots of trees. It is a very expensive food.

You have to make a choice now. You can get on a plane and go home. Or you can stay and explore more of France. There's still lots to see and do. There are many regions that you haven't visited yet. Will you stay, or go home?

Your plane is ready for take-off at Charles de Gaulle airport near Paris.

## Go truffle hunting

**Truffles** are edible **fungi** that grow underground or around the roots of trees. Fungi are plant-like growths such as mushrooms or mould. Truffles taste delicious and are very expensive to buy. Truffle hunters use specially trained pigs or dogs to sniff out the truffles.

A terrier gets a pat on the head from his owner. He has sniffed out a huge handful of truffles.

**fungus (plural: fungi)** organism that spreads over matter and absorbs it. Types of fungi include moulds and mushrooms.

# Find out more

## World Wide Web

If you want to find out more about France, you can search the Internet using keywords such as these:

- Paris
- River Seine
- The European Union.

You can also find your own keywords by using words from this book. Try using a search directory such as **www.yahooligans. com**.

## Movies

*Chocolat* (2000)
A hit movie about a Frenchwoman who opens a chocolate shop in a village.

*Belleville Rendez-Vous* (2003)
A cartoon about a kidnapped French cyclist.

You can find out more about France using the books, websites, and addresses listed below:

## The French Embassy

The French **Embassy** in your own country has lots of information about France. The UK embassy address is:

French Consulate General
6a Cromwell Place,
London SW7 2EN.

One of the best embassy websites is for the French Embassy in the United States:

**www.info-france-usa.org**.

## Further reading

*France (Focus on Europe)*, Anita Ganeri
  (Franklin Watts, 2004)

*France: Horrible Histories Special*, Terry Deary
  (Scholastic Hippo, 2004)

*Take Your Camera: France*, Ted Park
  (Raintree, 2004)

*The Rough Guide to France,* (Rough Guides, 2005)

revolution  replacing a government with a new one, usually by force

# Timeline

**58 BC to AD 476**
The Romans conquer Celtic Gaul (part of what is now called France).

**11th to 13th centuries**
The royal family and the religious leaders are the most powerful groups in France.

**14th to 15th centuries**
Rivalry between France and England leads to the Hundred Years' War.

**1610–1715**
Royal power is strongest during the reigns of French kings Louis XIII and Louis XIV.

**1789–1799**
The French **Revolution** takes power from the king. The king is executed in 1793.

**1799–1815**
Napoleon Bonaparte rises to power and becomes emperor of France.
France controls large areas of Europe.
Napoleon loses power in 1815.

**1815–1848**
Kings rule France once more.
Modern **industry** starts to appear.

**1848–1852**
There is a revolution and Louis Napoleon Bonaparte becomes President.

**1852–1870**
Louis Napoleon Bonaparte seizes power.
He rules France as Emperor Napoleon III.
France becomes more powerful.

**1870–1871**
France is at war with Prussia. Prussia was a European kingdom in north-central Europe. Napoleon III falls from power and France is defeated.

**1914–1918**
During World War I, Germany invades northern France.
Germany is defeated in 1918.

**1939–1945**
World War II.
German forces occupy France in 1940.
France is freed by May 1945.

**1946–1957**
France rebuilds itself after the war. Its overseas lands become **independent**.

**1968**
In May 1968, students and many workers go on strike. They protest against the government of General de Gaulle.

**1969–1981**
France becomes a leading member of the European Community. This organization was set up to improve trade between countries.

**January 1, 2002**
The Euro becomes the currency of France, and many other European countries.

---

**independent** when a country is free from control of another country

# France – facts and figures

The French flag, or "Tricolore" (three-colour), was created during the French Revolution. The three colours symbolize the monarchy (white) and the city of Paris (blue and red). It became the national flag in 1794, making it one of the world's oldest flags.

## People and places

- Population: 60 million
- Average life expectancy: 78.5 years
- The French have more pets than any other nationality. 25% have one or more cats, 38% have a dog.

## What's in a name?

- France's official name is République Française.
- France used to be called Gaul, but was invaded by the Franks in AD 400, and has been called France ever since.

## Money matters

- Before converting to the euro in 2002, France's currency was the French franc, made up of 100 centimes.
- Average earnings:
Men – £17,099 (US$30,022)
Women – £10,659 (US$18,715).

## Food facts

- France produces 20% of the world's wine.
- The French make over 400 different types of cheese.

# Glossary

**abbey** building used by people who belong to a religious order

**abseiling** using climbing rope to come down a steep hill or cliff face

*autoroute* French motorway designed for high-speed traffic

**Basque** people who live on the slopes of the Pyrenees mountains. They have their own language and way of life.

**border** imaginary line dividing one country from another

**canyon** deep valley with steep sides that has been formed by running water

**catacombs** tunnels used as burial chambers

**chalet** type of wooden house common in the Alps

**Channel Tunnel** railway tunnel under the English Channel

**embassy** place where another country has an official building

**English Channel** part of the Atlantic Ocean that separates France and the United Kingdom

**fungus (plural: fungi)** organism that spreads over matter and absorbs it. Types of fungi include moulds and mushrooms.

**funicular** railway that climbs up a very steep hill, pulled by cables

**gorge** steep-sided river valley

**heatwave** time of unusually hot weather

**immigrant** someone who originally comes from a different country

**independent** when a country is free from control of another country

**industry** businesses that provide a particular service

**kayaker** someone who paddles a small, light boat like a canoe through water

**memorial** something, such as a monument, that remembers or celebrates a person or an event

**Métro** Paris underground train system

**pollution** release of harmful chemicals and other substances into the air, ground, or water

**poverty** lack of money, a good home, or enough to eat

**rai** type of music originally from western Algeria

**revolution** replacing a government with a new one, usually by force

**seafood** fish, such as cod, and shellfish, such as crabs and mussels

**TGV (*train à grande vitesse*)** French high-speed train

**truffle** fleshy fungus that grows underground or around the roots of trees. It is a very expensive food.

**valley** area of lowland between hills or mountains

**voyage** long journey

**white-water rafter** someone who paddles or rows a raft along a fast-moving river with a strong current

# Index

# Titles in the *Destination Detectives* series include:

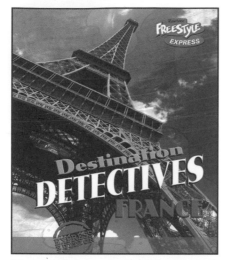

Hardback      1 406 20400 5

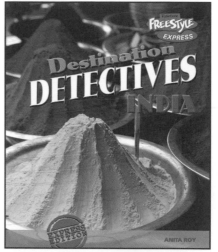

Hardback      1 406 20401 3

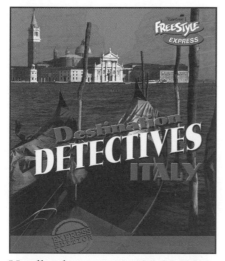

Hardback      1 406 20402 1

Hardback      1 406 20403 X

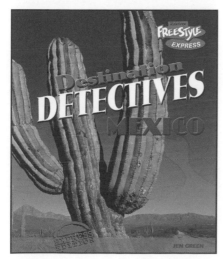

Hardback      1 406 20404 8

Hardback      1 406 20405 6

Find out about the other titles in this series on our website www.raintreepublishers.co.uk